Acting Edition

Theater Masters' Take Ten Volume 10

The Moon is Upside Down
by Comfort Ifeoma Katchy

The Quiet Rule
by Connor Johnson

Usurpations
by Natalie Lambert

Carrots
by Ally Merkel

2052
by Gretchen Suárez-Peña

The Courtship Ritual of Sandhill Cranes
by Emma Watkins

‖SAMUEL FRENCH‖

Introduction Copyright © 2025
The Moon is Upside Down © 2025 by Comfort Ifeoma Katchy
The Quiet Rule © 2025 by Connor Johnson
Usurpations © 2025 by Natalie Lambert
Carrots © 2025 by Ally Merkel
2052 © 2025 by Gretchen Suárez-Peña
The Courtship Ritual of Sandhill Cranes © 2025 by Emma Watkins
All Rights Reserved

THEATER MASTERS' TAKE TEN VOLUME 10 is fully protected under the copyright laws of the United States of America, the British Commonwealth, including Canada, and all member countries of the Berne Convention for the Protection of Literary and Artistic Works, the Universal Copyright Convention, and/or the World Trade Organization conforming to the Agreement on Trade Related Aspects of Intellectual Property Rights. All rights, including professional and amateur stage productions, recitation, lecturing, public reading, motion picture, radio broadcasting, television, online/digital production, and the rights of translation into foreign languages are strictly reserved.

ISBN 978-0-573-71167-1

www.concordtheatricals.com
www.concordtheatricals.co.uk

FOR PRODUCTION INQUIRIES

UNITED STATES AND CANADA
info@concordtheatricals.com
1-866-979-0447

UNITED KINGDOM AND EUROPE
licensing@concordtheatricals.co.uk
020-7054-7298

Each title is subject to availability from Concord Theatricals Corp., depending upon country of performance. Please be aware that *THEATER MASTERS' TAKE TEN VOLUME 10* may not be licensed by Concord Theatricals Corp. in your territory. Professional and amateur producers should contact the nearest Concord Theatricals Corp. office or licensing partner to verify availability.

CAUTION: Professional and amateur producers are hereby warned that *THEATER MASTERS' TAKE TEN VOLUME 10* is subject to a licensing fee. The purchase, renting, lending or use of this book does not constitute a license to perform this title(s), which license must be obtained from Concord Theatricals Corp. prior to any performance. Performance of this title(s) without a license is a violation of federal law and may subject the producer and/or presenter of such performances to civil penalties.

Both amateurs and professionals considering a production are strongly advised to apply to the appropriate agent before starting rehearsals, advertising, or booking a theatre. A licensing fee must be paid whether the title(s) is presented for charity or gain and whether or not admission is charged. Professional/Stock licensing fees are quoted upon application to Concord Theatricals Corp.

This work is published by Samuel French, an imprint of Concord Theatricals Corp.

No one shall make any changes in this title(s) for the purpose of production. No part of this book may be reproduced, stored in a retrieval system, scanned, uploaded, or transmitted in any form, by any means, now known or yet to be invented, including mechanical, electronic, digital, photocopying, recording, videotaping, or otherwise, without the prior written permission of the publisher. No one shall share this title(s), or any part of this title(s), through any social media or file hosting websites.

For all inquiries regarding motion picture, television, online/digital and other media rights, please contact Concord Theatricals Corp.

MUSIC AND THIRD-PARTY MATERIALS USE NOTE

Licensees are solely responsible for obtaining formal written permission from copyright owners to use copyrighted music and/or other copyrighted third-party materials (e.g. artworks, logos) in the performance of this play and are strongly cautioned to do so. If no such permission is obtained by the licensee, then the licensee must use only original music and materials that the licensee owns and controls. Licensees are solely responsible and liable for clearances of all third-party copyrighted materials, including without limitation music, and shall indemnify the copyright owners of the play(s) and their licensing agent, Concord Theatricals Corp., against any costs, expenses, losses and liabilities arising from the use of such copyrighted third-party materials by licensees. For music, please contact the appropriate music licensing authority in your territory for the rights to any incidental music.

IMPORTANT BILLING AND CREDIT REQUIREMENTS

If you have obtained performance rights to this title, please refer to your licensing agreement for important billing and credit requirements.

THEATER MASTERS STAFF & BOARD

Program Director: Emily Zemba
Executive Artistic Director: Victoria Hansen
Artistic Administrator: Lulu Guzman
Founder & Artistic Advisor: Julia Hansen

Board of Directors: Julia Hansen (President), Victoria Hansen, Naomi McDougall Jones, Amy Rose Marsh, Nancy Stevens, Charlotte Tripplehorn, Daisy Walker, Susan Lyons

National Advisory Board: Chris Ashley, Alec Baldwin, Andre Bishop, Scott Ellis, Doug Hughes, Judy Kaye, Andrew Leynse,* John Lithgow, Robert Moss, Brian Murray, Jack O'Brien, Neil Pepe, Theresa Rebeck, John Rando, Tim Sanford, A.R. Gurney,* Gordon Davidson*

2024 Creative Team
Directors: victor cervantes jr., Julie Kramer
Stage Manager: Kat Sloan Garcia
Casting: Sujotta Pace
Production Design: Stephen Cedars
Stage Directions read by: Lulu Guzman

2024 National Adjudicator
Lauren Yee

Thanks to all our Wonder Week guests and Friends of Theater Masters:
Abbie Van Nostrand, Amy Rose Marsh, Garrett Anderson, Rachel Levens, Ella Andrew, Ben Keiper, Faith Williams, Michael Bulger, Emily Morse, John Steber, Mark Orsini, Bonnie Davis, Michael Walkup, Michael Finkle, Luke Virkstis, Emma Feiwel, Lizzy Weingold, R.J. Tolan, Alex Barnett, Jessica Lit, Ioana Preda Buburuzan, Emmanuel Wilson, Noah Ezell, Beth Blickers, Katy Zapanta, Kaaron Briscoe, Beth Whitaker, Susan Bernfield, Salma Zohdi, Jessica Huang, Steph Del Rosso, Michael Mitnick, Meredith McDonough, Zach Ezer, Emily Dzioba, Lauren Yee, Broadway Green Alliance
...and so many more!

To learn more or donate, please visit theatermasters.org

---

emeritus

TABLE OF CONTENTS

Foreword	vi
The Moon is Upside Down	1
The Quiet Rule	23
Usurpations	41
Carrots	57
2052	71
The Courtship Ritual of Sandhill Cranes	87

FOREWORD

You are holding in your hands *Take Ten Volume 10*: a collection of six dynamic short plays by the winners of Theater Masters' 2024 National MFA Playwrights Competition. This anthology includes playwrights from University of Arkansas, Carnegie Mellon University, David Geffen School of Drama at Yale, New York University, UCLA, and UT Austin.

This year's plays offer deep explorations of faith, friendship, and love, through characters and situations that we think will genuinely surprise and engage you. The authors behind the texts are at the forefront of their field, and we're honored to have been able to meet them and their work at this early stage in their careers through these bold new plays.

The National MFA Playwrights Competition and the Take Ten Festival were founded in 2007 in order to bridge the gap between academic training and professional careers for emerging playwrights. Take Ten's professional development opportunities and partnership with Concord Theatricals have provided more than a hundred playwrights with a career-igniting entrance into the entertainment industry, while introducing their voices to the landscape of the American theater.

Take Ten 2024 was another success for Theater Masters. The six MFA playwrights joined us for a jam-packed two weeks of professional meetings, panels with industry professionals, Zoom meet-and-greets with agents, literary managers, artistic directors, and producers, and rehearsals for their ten-minute plays. Our incredible Take Ten 2024 directors victor cervantes jr. and Julie Kramer led the playwrights through thrilling, fast, and wildly productive workshops of their plays – culminating in a public reading presentation. Our stellar cast – delivered to us via our dedicated casting director Sujotta Pace – brought superb actors to the stage, and our designer Stephen Cedars made it possible for audiences to experience the full potential of each play beyond music stands. Our friends at Theatre Row were hosts to the evening of funny, tragic, and highly theatrical short plays. It was truly a hit!

Lauren Yee, our 2024 National Adjudicator, closed out the program as a mentor to our playwrights. Lauren expertly led a group "artistic matchmaking" session: guiding the writers through a brainstorm on writing, values, and career goals; helping each playwright craft a personalized list of potential theaters, partners, directors, and locales to pursue for their work.

We would like to thank our donors, supportive Board of Directors, and the many artists, industry leaders, and Theater Masters Alumni whose time and expertise helped to make Take Ten 2024 possible.

And finally: thank you for picking up this anthology and engaging with these unique theatrical voices.

Sincerely,
Emily Zemba, *Take Ten Program Director*
Vicky Hansen, *Executive Artistic Director*

The Moon is Upside Down

Comfort Ifeoma Katchy

THE MOON IS UPSIDE DOWN was first produced by Theater Masters in New York City on April 26th, 2024. The performance was directed by victor cervantes jr. The cast was as follows:

SHARON...Carmen Zilles
MEGAN......................................Jada Alston Owens

CHARACTERS

SHARON – 16, female
MEGAN – 26, female

SETTING

A van.

(We are in the back of a white Ford Econoline Van – **MEGAN** *and* **SHARON***'s wrists are tied behind their backs. The only light present in the van has been gifted by the moon –)*

(The van has been bouncing along for hours.)

*(****MEGAN*** *and* ***SHARON*** *are extremely exhausted.)*

SHARON. Can we stop for a second

please

My head hurts

MEGAN. OK

SHARON. I don't think any of those ideas are gonna work

MEGAN. They might

(Beat.)

SHARON. The bumping is making my stomach hurt

MEGAN. Are you going to throw up again

SHARON. I don't think so

MEGAN. Good

It already smells bad

(Beat.)

SHARON. I hope we stop soon

He has to pee at some point

MEGAN. True

Unless he's one of those people that can hold their pee for obscene amounts of time

MEGAN. I can hold mine for a really long time

But this is a really long time

But maybe he's wearing a diaper

That sounds practical

SHARON. I'm realizing something about myself right now

MEGAN. What's that

SHARON. I get very angry when I'm annoyed

MEGAN. Am I annoying you

SHARON. Yes

No

MEGAN. Sorry

    (Beat.)

I get angry when I get annoyed too

    (Beat.)

SHARON. I have to pee

MEGAN. You should pee on yourself

SHARON. Why

MEGAN. If he comes back here and if he tries to pick you up

You can rub your pee on him

SHARON. How would I do that

MEGAN. Take off your pants I don't know

SHARON. *Why* would I do that

MEGAN. I don't know

No one likes pee rubbed on them

SHARON. Some people do

MEGAN. Oh

That's gross

SHARON. Yeah

I'll hold it

MEGAN. How long can you hold your pee

SHARON. I don't know

MEGAN. I can hold mine for a really long time. I've always held my pee. That's why I never stop for a public bathroom. Well. That. And public bathrooms creep me out. So I always hold my pee.

SHARON. Why do public bathrooms creep you out

MEGAN. I saw that movie *Saw*

You know the one with the clown and that guy that has to saw off his own foot – I wonder if that's why they named it that. Anyways I saw that movie when I was too young to be watching movies like that. And so bathrooms have always creeped me out since

SHARON. That movie is creepy

MEGAN. Yeah –

But

That's why I hate going to public bathrooms

I always panic on the inside

SHARON. Oh

I'm sorry

I just

I really had to pee

MEGAN. I know

And I wanted cheetos

(Beat.)

SHARON. Are there any left

MEGAN. Cheetos

SHARON. Yeah

MEGAN. Let me check

No

*(**SHARON** lets out a frustrated scream.)*

(Beat.)

Do you wanna pray

SHARON. What

MEGAN. Pray

SHARON. For what

MEGAN. For us

SHARON. Oh

Yeah

Sure

MEGAN. Okay

Do you wanna go

SHARON. I said yeah

MEGAN. Like

Do you wanna start

Start the prayer

SHARON. But it was your idea

MEGAN. Yeah I know

But I just like to ask

Because

You never know

You might like praying

    (Pause.)

Do you like praying

SHARON. Yeah

MEGAN. What do you believe about praying

SHARON. That's a question I've never been asked

MEGAN. Yeah

I'm good at that

Asking questions

Random questions I guess

Sometimes people think I'm weird for asking so many questions

But you learn a lot about a person

From asking questions that are kinda off the wall

SHARON. Yeah –

MEGAN. So what do you believe about praying

SHARON. That

Uhm

God hears us

What do you believe about praying

MEGAN. That God hears us

I believe He really loves us

Like a lot a lot

And wants to know us

MEGAN. And for us to know Him

And because He cares He knows what we need

And responds accordingly

Because He knows all

And He loves us

So it's like

Praying is us being able to talk to God

Honestly

And free of judgment

You know

SHARON. Yeah

MEGAN. I like talking to Him like He's my father

SHARON. Yeah

I talk to Him like He's my friend

MEGAN. I believe He always answers our prayers

Not always the way we expect

But He does

SHARON. Yeah

MEGAN. So what do you talk to Him about

SHARON. Everything

MEGAN. Like what

SHARON. Like

Should I do this

Or

Should I do that

MEGAN. Like what

SHARON. Like

Should I do

This

Or should

I do

That

MEGAN. But like what

SHARON. Like should I move to New York City and try to become a famous actress

Or stay here in Texas and buy a farm

MEGAN. I want a farm

SHARON. Yeah

MEGAN. I want lots of cows

And goats

Like baby goats

SHARON. I want pigs

Teacup pigs

MEGAN. Those are cute

SHARON. Yeah

(Beat.)

MEGAN. Do you wanna pray

SHARON. Oh –

Yeah

MEGAN. You can go first

SHARON. Okay

Uhm

SHARON. Hey God

    Jesus

    Lord and Savior

    How's it going

    Being Holy

    Ruling the world

    It's a good world You've made

    So thank You

    I'm grateful to be a part of it

    Uhm

    So

    My friend

    And

    I

    Are –

    Have been

    Are kidnapped.

    We're in the back of a van

    It might be my fault

    And I'm sorry

    Forgive me.

    But we're scared

    Heart-in-my-throat-pounding-hard-scared

    And we would really like to be safe

    God

    Lord

Jesus

Christ

Mighty Savior

Uhm

We're scared

And need You

Uhm

To do something

Anything

Like

A flat tire

Or

I don't know

Anything to help

Please help

Amen

MEGAN. Lord

I'm sorry for sinning

Lying to my parents

Having sex with –

Smoking weed

I know one of those reasons

Or maybe all of them

Are probably why I'm here

In the back of a van

I'm not sure

MEGAN. But I'm sorry

I want to do the right thing

Be righteous

And allathat

But

It's hard

There's so much

Temptation

Down here

I know You know

But

Living down here is hard

And scary sometimes

Like now

I know Sharon told You we're in the back of a van

And it smells

Really bad

And maybe

Maybe You could open a window

Or

Something

That would help

But

Uhm

Yeah

Can You send Your Holy Spirit to comfort us

That would help too

Thanks for listening

In Jesus' bless-ed name we pray

>   (**MEGAN** *bows her head.*)

Amen

SHARON. Amen.

>   *(Beat.)*

MEGAN. So

I guess

Now

We wait

SHARON. What?

MEGAN. Well

I know God heard our prayer

So

Now

We wait

>   *(Beat.)*

SHARON. Do you really think He's heard our prayer

MEGAN. Yeah

SHARON. Will He do anything

MEGAN. I think so

He helped David out

Do you feel Him?

SHARON. No

   Do you

MEGAN. I think so

SHARON. I feel fear

   And confusion

   And

   Maybe a dead rat but I don't wanna know for sure

MEGAN. I feel Him

   Jesus can you get us out of here

   We're scared

   We're scared

      (Beat.)

   This morning I was really scared

   Almost more scared than I am now

   I thought I was pregnant

   I told God if He made me not pregnant

   I'd start going to church again

   Then I got my period

   That's when I texted you

      (Beat.)

   Are you a virgin

SHARON. No

   But I'm celibate

MEGAN. Why

SHARON. I wanna save myself

   For my husband

MEGAN. Does that still count

Like

'Cause

You're not a virgin

SHARON. I think so

MEGAN. Oh

So yeah

God really came through for me this morning

I know He'll do it again

SHARON. How

How do you know

MEGAN. He promised.

>   *(Beat.)*

>   *(**MEGAN** hums a hymn to herself.*)*

>   *(Beat.)*

SHARON. My heart isn't pounding as hard

MEGAN. Mine either

>   *(Beat.)*

Thank you for picking me up

For Bible study

I know we didn't make it there

But thank you for coming to get me

It means a lot

---

* A license to produce *The Moon Is Upside Down* does not include a performance license for any third-party or copyrighted music. Licensees should create an original composition or use music in the public domain. For further information, please see the Music and Third-Party Materials Use Note on page iii.

SHARON. It's not a problem at all

Not having a car in Houston sucks

I know what it's like

MEGAN. Yeah

Not having friends sucks more

SHARON. I know what that's like too

MEGAN. Yeah

   (Beat.)

Why did you invite me to church

I'm really grateful

But

I just started working at Applebee's like a week ago

And I thought for sure you didn't like me 'cause I talk too much

But you barely know me

SHARON. Yeah

I know

I just

It's 'cause

I saw

I see

A lot of myself

Of me

In you

When I was your age

MEGAN. How old are you

SHARON. Twenty-six

MEGAN. You're twenty-six?!

Are you milking my cow

SHARON. What

No

I'm twenty-six

MEGAN. What

I thought you were

At most

nineteen

I'm sixteen

SHARON. Yeah

I know

MEGAN. That's crazy

You look good for twenty-six

SHARON. Thanks

    (Beat.)

MEGAN. So do you ever feel like a you're a loser for working at Applebee's

Like I always thought when I'm twenty-six, I'd be making a lot of money – not that we don't make a lot of money at Applebee's but I never saw it as a real job like I'm still in high school so it's okay that I'm working there but like you're twenty-six do you ever feel like you're a loser

Like

No offense

I was just wondering

SHARON. Uhm

>Sometimes
>
>But
>
>I also believe I'm where I'm supposed to be
>
>In life
>
>I don't think I'll be here forever
>
>But
>
>I'm here now
>
>And I'm grateful
>
>Well
>
>In life
>
>Not here
>
>Here I'm not –
>
>My heart's pounding so hard
>
>I'm so scared
>
>What if we don't get rescued

MEGAN. We have to

>We will
>
>We are
>
>Jesus is here
>
>Right

SHARON. Yeah

>He is
>
>He always is

MEGAN. Okay

>Holy Spirit you are welcome here

*(A small white light appears inside the van, Unnoticed by the **GIRLS**.)*

(Beat.)

He's here

Do you feel Him

SHARON. Yeah

I do.

Holy Spirit you are welcome here

MEGAN. Holy Spirit you are welcome here

(The light grows larger and larger.)

(Beat.)

SHARON. I don't feel scared

MEGAN. He's here.

(The white light has grown large, encompassing the van.)

(The van bounces along.)

(Lights fade.)

(Sounds of sirens.)

(Blackout.)

The Quiet Rule

Connor Johnson

THE QUIET RULE was first produced by Theater Masters in New York City on April 26th, 2024. The performance was directed by Julie Kramer. The cast was as follows:

GEORGIA ....Danielle Skrastaad

CHARACTERS

GEORGIA – Female, any age, no longer believes in the quiet rule.

SETTING

A public library.

TIME

Just before closing.

AUTHOR'S NOTE

Locations should be suggested, no need for realistic sets.

(**GEORGIA** *is at the library.*)

(She stands upon a table, declaiming:)

GEORGIA. Hello people of the library.

So –

So I just wanted to say I'm sorry.

Because –

Because I was wrong.

Because –

Because there is no such thing as the quiet rule.

I used to believe.

I used to believe in the quiet rule –

But now I don't anymore.

I don't believe in the quiet rule anymore.

And I want to apologize to you all for the intense hatred I've secretly felt for each of you if you were making noise while I was writing.

And all the times I wrote in my journal "fuck you fuck you stop talking about coffee."

And I will say –

It did seem,

Recently,

That every time I was here,

At least one of you was making noise.

Maybe a woman in a zoom meeting,

Or a guy with a white handlebar mustache listening to AC/DC,

Or a couple talking in low tones.

To attempt to make it less distracting,

But actually,

That actually makes it more distracting,

Because low tones draw the ear.

Because it makes it something I shouldn't be listening to.

Which only makes me want to listen more.

Rating the library coffee in low tones:

"The drip is no good"

That sort of thing,

"Oh, you should try the cortado"

"Cortado?"

"Yeah."

"What's that?"

"It's a cappuccino but with less milk"

"You mean a macchiato?"

"No. A macchiato is just a little foam on top. A cortado has more milk."

"Oh."

"Yeah."

...

"But less than a cappuccino?"

"Yeah."

"But…how much less? 'Cause I feel like a cappuccino is already fairly low on milk."

"Sure."

"I mean, that's kinda the whole point right?"

"What is?"

"It's an alternative to a latte."

"Okay."

…

"Wait – I think that person – they're sitting over there –"

"What?"

"That person, right there, ahead of us, you see them?"

"Yeah."

"I think that person is listening to us, and writing down what we are saying,"

"What?"

"They're –

Yeah,

I think they're writing down

What I'm saying right now.

I'm gonna –

You stay here,

I'm gonna try to get closer,

See if I can tell,

See if I can see what they are typing.

See if it's really us."

And he slowly extracts himself from his chair.

And he silently tiptoes behind me,

And the hairs on the back of my neck stand up...
Wait –
Am I turned on by this?
But no,
I'm not turned on,
It's my hackles,
My hackles.
My hackles are raised,
But then –
What's that?!
A soft and small shuffle behind me.
Someone's there,
Not too close to touch,
But close enough to sense,
Maybe,
If auras are real,
Our auras are touching,
Little bubbles softening at their edges,
Threatening to pop.
And now he's right behind me,
Looking over my shoulder,
At what I'm typing.
And he's breathing over my shoulder.
I can hear his breath in his mouth,
Hot and sharp.
And I think I can feel it,

On the back of my neck,

Or maybe it's his aura

Or maybe its only my erect hairs –

Maybe because they are erect

They reach out far enough

To pluck the breath

From the mouth

Of this person.

And maybe he says:

"Hey –

That's me,

That's what I'm doing"

And I say:

"Yes."

And he pauses,

And he reads what I've written,

And he says:

"I sound pretty good,

In this,

You've made me sound

Pretty cool."

And I say:

"Oh –

Thanks"

"Sexy,

Kinda"

"Oh – I don't know."

"Yeah,

I think you do,

'Erect hairs'

I mean,

Come on"

"Oh,

Well,

Yeah,

Yeah,

It is a bit…

Sexy."

His arm on my shoulder,

"I like that,

How you've written me."

Squeeze.

"Yeah?"

"It's good"

"Oh yeah?"

"Yeah"

"Well."

"Well well."

Tighter squeeze.

"I wanna

Fuck you

Right here

In this library"

And I say:

"Oh?

Really?"

"Yeah.

You want to?"

"I –

I...

...yes..."

And he kisses my neck from behind.

And my hairs go even more erect,

And then his hand reaches around to cup my breast,

And then he says:

"Actually maybe we should go somewhere else,

'Cause my girlfriend is sitting right over there."

And I say:

"Where do you have in mind?

I have to get some work done

At some point."

And he says:

"There's a church right across the street."

"A church?"

"A church."

"Are you sure?"

"Yeah why not?"

"Isn't that sort of sacrilegious?"

"What are you?

A priest?"

And I'm not a priest,

So he led me to this church,

And we went inside,

And inside it was quiet,

And still.

And I thought:

"Fuck I should have brought my work with me to do in this church."

And he said:

"Lay back on this pew."

And I did.

…

He started at my ear –

His breath hot and sharp in my ear tube,

His tongue wide and wet.

His nose navigated my body,

Down my neck,

Across my breasts,

Inside my knee socket,

He smelled me attentively.

And yes,

It was a red flag,

But also,

I was into it.

And as he fumbled with my belt I laid my head back on the hardwood pew.

And as he undid my waist buttons I drank in the silence of that church.

And as his fingers curled in the hem of my jeans and under the waistband of my undies and as his body tensed to tear them both off together in one barbaric yank there suddenly erupted from the back of the church a cacophonous thunderous horrible groan –

An organ!

Someone was here and that someone was playing the organ!

Or probably actually learning the organ because they were terrible –

Truly very bad at the organ.

And,

And it was,

It was such a...

Violation!

You know?

A violation of the silence of this church!

This stupid shitty organ playing,

You could hear them,

Counting out the music under their breath,

And they were still fucking up the rhythm!

And my new lover,

Well,

He looked up from my body with utter contempt in the direction of this –

This –

Amateur organist!

And he stood up with violence,

And he turned to the door,

And he left,

In a hurry,

Without a word,

In a flight of disgust.

And then I was alone.

Well not alone,

It was me and this amateur organist,

Ruining this music,

Ruining this church,

Ruining my life.

But I couldn't go back

To my work.

I couldn't go back

To this couple,

To this man who I'd nearly adulterated with.

So I was stuck.

Listening to this this –

Lay organist

Bumble their way through this music,

Which is supposed to be beautiful,

I mean –

That's the whole point,

Right?

But here's this –

This…

Hobbyist organist!

Repeating the phrases where they made mistakes,

Just to go back and make them again.

And I wanted to explode right then and there I wanted to explode so hard that my atoms would never find a way to rejoin themselves and reform my body and my brain and my conscious.

But then,

Suddenly,

The music stopped.

And a delicate silence suspended itself across the church,

Like dust drifting in light,

Drifting in the light beaming from the church windows,

Green, gold, and blue stripes.

And the church was dim,

And the silence was dim,

Earthen and dim like

A woods' hollow in winter

After a snowfall,

Soft and unwrinkled.

Quiet like a box.

(Long silence.)

And then slowly,

This –

This –

This…

Organist.

With audible hesitation,

Stretched their inexperienced fingers back to the organ's keys,

And I braced myself for imminent aural aggravation,

However,

Instead,

As they began to play,

The light from the window

Green, gold and blue stripes,

Was unmistakably audible

In the notes from the pipes.

    (Beat.)

And after a while I stood up,

And walked out of the church,

And back across the street,

To the library,

To my work.

And the couple was gone,

And another couple

Had taken its place,

Talking in low tones.

And a man with a white handlebar mustache was listening to AC/DC,

And a woman was on a work meeting on her laptop,

But now,

Now these sounds,

These voices,

Were suffused with light.

And I sat in my chair,

And I closed my eyes,

And felt the light on my eyelids,

And it was nice,

It was nice,

To just sit.

And I didn't get any work done at all.

>   *(***GEORGIA*** sits back down.)*
>
>   *(Far away, the sound of an organ is heard.)*

Usurpations

Natalie Lambert

USURPATIONS was first produced by Theater Masters in New York City on April 26th, 2024. The performance was directed by victor cervantes jr. The cast was as follows:

WRISTWATCH .... Milo Longnecker
TARGET..Emiliano Morales
WADDA..Shayvawn Webster
KALLA...Jennifer Pillaga
DOGGY .... Frankie A. Rodriguez
CARRIE .... Karma Alami

CHARACTERS

WRISTWATCH – fourteen, a boy
TARGET – fourteen, a boy
WADDA – twelve, a girl
KALLA – eleven, a girl
DOGGY – eight, a boy
CARRIE – eight, a girl

SETTING

A forest in the United States of America.

TIME

An apocalypse.

AUTHOR'S NOTES

// indicates the beginning of the next line of dialogue

(A group of kids in a forest. It is night. There is a fire lit. They sit on logs, or on the ground. A dog, Boy, sits next to them.)

(They are staring at a whiteboard with the word "Usurpations" written on it.)

(The first few moments of this play live in slow motion. Consider elongating the first two words.)

(If I was conducting, my hands would go down on "what" and "the" with both words being held for two beats.)

(The rest of the line, and the following dialogue, should jump to a quick and frenetic tempo, like a regurgitation of all of human history happening at once.)

WRISTWATCH. What.

The.

FUCK am I even looking at right now!

KALLA. I am promising, I have seen it before!

TARGET. She's making fuck up again.

KALLA. That was one time and I was OBLIVIOUSLY joking!

WRISTWATCH. She's right. That word was obliviously fake. How would you even use "Google" in a sentence?

*(**WADDA** is flipping through a binder.)*

TARGET. Wadda, something yet?

WADDA. Nope, not yet.

WRISTWATCH. What was the sentence?

KALLA. I said I can not memember!

WRISTWATCH. It's just one of those words that are ugly to look at. Like you!

TARGET. We change it. Take out "r."

DOGGY. Should mean "silly!"

KALLA. I think it should mean "ugly."

WADDA. Let's see if we can find the meaning before we change anything.

TARGET. She's damning with us.

KALLA. Am not!

WADDA. We'll come back to this one, this is taking too long. Wristwatch. Go ahead.

> *(He flips the whiteboard to the other side. Everyone gathers around the whiteboard.)*

KALLA. Knife?

> *(**TARGET** passes her a knife. **KALLA** cuts her hand and bleeds into a bowl. The others gather around, and capture the blood into their fountain pens. **DOGGY** feeds Boy some food.)*

WADDA. Doggy, it's your turn to bleed next.

WRISTWATCH. He's eight. I'll bleed for him.

> *(**WADDA** stares at him.)*

Wadda, we just found him two weeks ago.

WADDA. No, *you* found him. You didn't even ask if you could bring him in.

Not like he's offered us a single meaning since he's been here.

WRISTWATCH. He brought us Boy!

KALLA. Yeah, here boy!

> (**KALLA** pets Boy. **WADDA** rolls her eyes.)

> (**WRISTWATCH** begins writing "Emigrate" on the board in red marker.)

WADDA. WRISTWATCH, THAT'S MY MARKER!

WRISTWATCH. I need three pens for this one.

WADDA. Give it back! Blue is my favorite.

WRISTWATCH. We'll find more blue!

WADDA. You can't even find us the white stuff that goes in our vaginas. Give it!

> (**WRISTWATCH** rolls his eyes and throws her the marker.)

WRISTWATCH. So I have three:

Emigrate. Immigrate. And Migrate.

> (**EVERYONE** writes in their notebook.)

Emigrate is to leave your country. Immigrate is to live in a new country. Migrate is to move from one part of something to another.

TARGET. So everyone's got jokes tonight.

> (**WRISTWATCH** pulls a piece of paper out of his pocket.)

WRISTWATCH. I'm not joking.

> (**WADDA** grabs the note. She turns the page over.)

I uh. I found it in someone's room.

(**WADDA** *struggles on the following words: "elementary," "order," and "story."*)

WADDA. "Katie's elementary school was burnt to a crisp. Our block is under order to stay inside.

To those who live. Tell our story."

...What the fuck is elementary?

TARGET. Mark in the log.

WADDA. Wristwatch this is too much, let's just use one of the words to mean all three.

WRISTWATCH. No! We have their meanings!

WADDA. And we're changing them, we need to conserve our pages.

KALLA. Which one are we keeping?

| **WRISTWATCH.** | **WADDA.** | **TARGET.** |
| Immigrate | Emigrate. | Migrate. |

WADDA. Marking this. We'll vote later. Who's next?

TARGET. I've not anything.

WADDA. Yeah. Me neither. Slow week.

WRISTWATCH. Let's keep my three then!

WADDA. No, Wristwatch. It's not... Kalla, what was that word you found last week?

KALLA. Efficient.

WADDA. Efficient, it's not efficient.

KALLA. Back to mine!

(**KALLA** *turns the board back over.* **DOGGY** *whispers in* **WRISTWATCH**'s *ear.*)

WADDA. Hey! If you're gonna talk, you have to talk to all of us!

WRISTWATCH. He's embarrassed about his words.

WADDA. Doggy, what'd you tell him?

DOGGY. ...Hungry

WADDA. Yeah well you shouldn't have fed Boy your dinner! Stupid ass.

TARGET. Take the book, get berries.

KALLA. He can not read stupid ass.

>(**WRISTWATCH** *grabs a book out of a backpack.*)

WRISTWATCH. Alright Doggy, look. See the berries on this page? Go pick them off the bushes. If they look like this

>(*He flips to another page.*)

they'll kill you. Do you know what kill means?

>(**DOGGY** *nods.*)

Alright, go.

WADDA. HEY! Memember to check it out!

>(**WADDA** *hands the check-out log to* **DOGGY**. *He stares at it.*)

WRISTWATCH. Go ahead Doggy. I'll check it out for you.

>(**DOGGY** *goes into the forest.* **WRISTWATCH** *signs his name.*)

You're a bitch Wadda.

>(**KALLA** *and* **TARGET** *giggle.*)

WADDA. What does – what does "bitch" mean?

WRISTWATCH. Lovely person.

>(*They giggle again.* **WADDA** *glares at them.*)

KALLA. Okay. Usurpations.

WRISTWATCH. Kalla if you're damning with us –

TARGET. Why care? Wadda will change it. She changed my word last week.

WADDA. "Saccharine" looks evil!

TARGET. It means sweet!

WADDA. We already voted to change it! And *I* am in charge of determining when we should vote on a change!

TARGET. Stop talking to me like that, I am more old than you are!

WADDA. So? I've brought in more meanings than you!

>   (*Rustling in the bushes.*)

Doggy?

>   (*No answer. More rustling. They grab their knives.*)

WRISTWATCH. Doggy? Doggy are you okay?

>   (**DOGGY** *stumbles out from the bushes. He's been stabbed.*)

DOGGY. Boy?

>   (*He falls.*)

>   (**KALLA** *screams.* **WRISTWATCH** *and* **TARGET** *run into the forest.*)

>   (*Boy runs after them.*)

WADDA. TARGET! FIND THE BOOK!

>   (**DOGGY** *falls to the ground.* **WADDA** *shakes him.*)

DOGGY THE BOOK! WHERE'S THE BOOK!

DOGGY. Took it.

(**WADDA** *runs into the forest.* **KALLA** *looks through bags to find medical supplies.*)

Kalla. Paper.

KALLA. No Doggy. You are going to be good.

DOGGY. Please.

KALLA. WADDA! GRAB DOGGY'S PAGE!!

(**WADDA** *runs in. She flips through the binder.*)

DOGGY. Sorry book tooken.

KALLA. Do not talk, Doggy.

(**WADDA** *runs over with a paper.*)

DOGGY. Kalla? Please.

(**KALLA** *grabs the paper and reads from it.*)

KALLA. Perra estúpida. Sé que besaste a mi hombre. Encuéntrame detrás de las gradas después de clase. Coño.

DOGGY. Don't eat Boy.

(**DOGGY** *dies.*)

WADDA. We never decided on those words.

KALLA. It is okay. He just liked the way they sound.

(**WRISTWATCH** *and* **TARGET** *carry on a screaming young* **GIRL.**)

CARRIE. PLEASE, PLEASE DON'T KILL ME!

(**WADDA** *grabs her bag and looks through it.*)

WRISTWATCH. WHERE ARE THEY?!

CARRIE. I'M ALONE! I SWEAR I'M ALONE!

*(***TARGET*** puts his knife to* ***CARRIE****'s throat.)*

PLEASE PLEASE PLEASE – wait why do you have usurpations written on that white board?

(Silence.)

KALLA. You – You know that word?

CARRIE. I've seen it. I think I might have the paper. Check towards the beginning.

*(***WADDA*** flips through her notebook. She struggles on the following words: "history," "present," "Britain," "repeated," "establishment," "absolute," and "tyranny.")*

WADDA. Here it is.

"The history of the present King of Great Britain is a history of repeated injuries and usurpations, all having in direct object the establishment of an absolute Tyranny over these States."

(Profound silence. ***TARGET****'s knife is still on* ***CARRIE****'s throat.)*

WRISTWATCH. What. The.

TARGET. FUCK is tyranny?!

KALLA. Establishment?!?!

WRISTWATCH. Great Britain???

WADDA. What does it mean?

CARRIE. I don't know.

KALLA. Well injuries is like when you hit your head. Great means very good.

TARGET. Wadda, where have I seen "King" before?

(**WADDA** *pulls out a Burger King sandwich wrapper from her binder.**)

WADDA. This paper that once held food!

KALLA. Okay. So. King means someone who makes food!

WRISTWATCH. This sentence makes no sense.

TARGET. Great. Thanks for nothing girl.

(**TARGET** *presses his knife deeper into* **CARRIE**'s *throat.*)

CARRIE. DON'T KILL ME! I-I-I know a lot of words!

My mom worked for The New York Times // she made puzzles. Crosswords.

WADDA. The New York Times?! The black and white paper company?

WRISTWATCH. We don't care how many words you know. Target. Do it.

CARRIE. NO NO NO – WHY ARE YOU NAMED AFTER THE RETAIL STORE?!?

TARGET. What? I found the word on a number and lines paper.

CARRIE. A receipt?

KALLA. What is a detail store?

TARGET. My name is cool everyone shut up!

WADDA. GUYS! She has a pencil!

KALLA. No way! Let me see.

WADDA. Where did you get this?

---

* A license to produce *Usurpations* does not include a license to publicly display any third-party or copyrighted images. Licensees must acquire rights for any copyrighted images or create their own.

CARRIE. My mom managed to save one. She gave it to me.

I really do know a lot of words. Their meanings are all in my head.

KALLA. Oh yeah? What is this one – Wadda what was your word last week?

WADDA. Distorted – here I'll write it.

> *(She writes it on the board. Everyone stares at **CARRIE**.)*

CARRIE. Uh. It means... Gross. Like, disgusting.

> *(Silence. They contemplate.)*

WADDA. I'll take it.

KALLA. Yeah I mean, I have no way of knowing.

TARGET. You have a mom? Where is she?

CARRIE. They killed her.

WADDA. Who? How old were they?

CARRIE. Ten? Eleven? They found us in a restaurant. I don't know which one. The sign was burnt. We were looking for menus. She said menus were some of the last of the papers to be burnt...

They shot her. It's not their fault. She's an adult.

WRISTWATCH. I don't believe her. If you have a pencil, why haven't you written down any meanings?

CARRIE. They're called definitions.

KALLA. What does definitions mean?

CARRIE. Definition means meaning.

WRISTWATCH. Meaning means meaning! We already have a word for it.

Why haven't you written your words down!

CARRIE. I'm eight, I still have good memory. I'm saving my pencil for when I need it. Don't kill me, I can – I can help keep your books!

WRISTWATCH. No.

WADDA. Wristwatch. You know we can't kill her. It's sad. About that Doggy guy. But she has a lot of words.

WRISTWATCH. Shut up Wadda, you stupid fucking bitch! I'll kill you!

WADDA. Kill me? Hah! Who's gonna keep our books if you kill me!

WRISTWATCH. I don't give a fuck I'll fucking kill you and keep the books myself!

WADDA. You can't kill me! That is a complete usurpation of power! Oh you know what, // I hear it now. When you say it in context – yeah I get it.

EVERYONE ELSE. Ohhhhhhhh.

Carrots

Ally Merkel

CARROTS was first produced by Theater Masters in New York City on April 26th, 2024. The performance was directed by Julie Kramer. The cast was as follows:

EVERETT...Hagan Oliveras
JACK..Savidu Geevaratne

CHARACTERS

EVERETT – 15. Boy.
JACK – 15. Boy.

SETTING

Somewhere near a basketball hoop, outside.

TIME

Present day.

AUTHOR'S NOTES

A slash (/) indicates an interruption.

(**EVERETT** and **JACK** *shoot hoops outside.*)

EVERETT. So Gavin is just walking around with half of his dick cut off?

JACK. I'm telling you that is what happened

EVERETT. She just – bit it off

JACK. Yep. Chomp.

EVERETT. No freakin way

JACK. Dude fuck yes!

EVERETT. Is there like, photo evidence circulating, or –

JACK. You mean like have I seen a picture of Gavin's dick?

EVERETT. Wait do you think he can even get hard anymore

JACK. Dude this is not the point

EVERETT. I'm just saying like I guess I wouldn't take a pic of my dick if I couldn't get hard anymore

JACK. Bro his ability to take a dick pic is not the point

The point is that like – she bit it off – just like with her with her with her MOUTH

EVERETT. Wow

JACK. Yes WOW thank you

EVERETT. I guess it must be like the carrot thing

JACK. Huh

EVERETT. You know how you can bite through your finger as easily as you can bite through a carrot

And the only reason we don't is cuz like our brain stops us from doing it

JACK. Oh yeah that's definitely true

EVERETT. Yeah.

JACK. Yeah

> *(They take turns shooting hoops for a moment.)*

Also on the topic of girls / and shit

EVERETT. I can't believe you leave tomorrow for the ENTIRE SUMMER

JACK. Yeah I know

EVERETT. It's like

I've seen you every day for the last 180 days or something

JACK. I don't even want to go to piano camp

EVERETT. I've been SAYING this –

JACK. I've been like

Trying to think of how I could get out of it in the next twenty-four hours honestly

EVERETT. I could bite your finger off

JACK. Literally please

EVERETT. Then we could like play basketball every single day

JACK. Yeah totally

And like also there's the element of like

With me and Grace happening and shit

EVERETT. Oh

Yeah

JACK. Yeah like because we've been like…

EVERETT. You've been hanging more?

JACK. Yeah well actually that's what I meant about girls and shit because I've been wanting to tell you or like I keep forgetting to tell you all day today but like yeah I asked her to be my girlfriend

EVERETT. Oh wow

JACK. Yeah I know

EVERETT. Yeah wow that's cool

JACK. Ha yeah thanks man

EVERETT. I didn't know you were hanging that much

JACK. Yeah I guess we have been

EVERETT. So when have you been hanging

JACK. You know like after school

EVERETT. Yeah but we hang every day after school so like when

JACK. Oh I guess like sometimes later

EVERETT. Like you sneak out?

JACK. Yeah once or twice I guess

EVERETT. I thought you didn't like sneaking out

JACK. I don't

EVERETT. But for vagina

JACK. Bro

EVERETT. No I mean like that's hot yeah

JACK. Okay

EVERETT. So do you have sex

JACK. Yeah
   Yeah
   Yeah

EVERETT. .

JACK. ...

EVERETT. .

JACK. No

We haven't

EVERETT. Yeah

JACK. But we're gonna

I mean we're really thinking about it

EVERETT. Oh yeah that's good

JACK. I just like

Like I keep trying to think of how I could convince my parents that it's okay if I quit piano –

EVERETT. Don't you think it's kind of dumb to quit piano for some girl

JACK. I mean you already know that like in general or whatever I've been doubting if I want to keep doing piano or if it's like all for my parents or whatever

EVERETT. Yeah but like

But like it's your extracurricular

JACK. Basketball is my extracurricular

EVERETT. I mean like it's the one that's gonna get you into college

JACK. Dude why are you thinking about college

EVERETT. I'm just saying it's important to show that you've committed to something for a long time

JACK. Uhm. Okay.

EVERETT. I guess I'm just surprised because like

Like how many times have you even hung out with Grace

JACK. A lot?

EVERETT. Like does she make you laugh

JACK. Yeah she's really funny

EVERETT. Okay cool.
She just never seemed that funny in class

JACK. Well that's class

EVERETT. Yeah I guess so

JACK. And anyways if I don't go to piano camp then you and I can hang out more, like you said

EVERETT. Yeah I guess if you're not busy trying to figure out how to get hard for Grace or whoever

JACK. Dude why do you do this weird shit every time I try to talk about girls

EVERETT. I'm not being weird I just don't like talking about girls

JACK. Have you ever considered, like, why –

EVERETT. Because there are more interesting things to talk about

JACK. Like what

EVERETT. Like all of the other things we talk about
We have a lot of other things to talk about

JACK. Okay sure
And maybe if you bit my finger off we could keep talking about all of those other things

EVERETT. Dude –

JACK. I was thinking about spraining my wrist

EVERETT. Bro I'm *not* biting your finger off –

JACK. Your brain would just think it was a carrot

EVERETT. I'm not biting your fucking finger off.

JACK. Because you want me to go to camp?

EVERETT. Because you're being psychotic

JACK. Fingers grow back

EVERETT. Since *when*

JACK. Come on

I know you want to

EVERETT. No I fucking don't want to

JACK. We can play basketball *every day*

EVERETT. You wouldn't even be able to play basketball every day because you wouldn't have a finger

JACK. So you would finally beat me.

EVERETT. I beat you.

JACK. Why are you being so jealous right now

EVERETT. I'm not jealous!

JACK. You're obviously jealous

EVERETT. I get girls

JACK. I don't know Evy

I don't know

I just feel like sometimes like

Look, I know that I'm like, your first best friend or whatever –

EVERETT. I've had friends

JACK. Not really

EVERETT. They just sucked but they were my friends

JACK. Yeah I know

EVERETT. Like they were just weird and emo and cut themselves and stuff but they were my friends

JACK. Okay sure

EVERETT. You are literally the one who asks me to hang out every day

JACK. Because you're always available

EVERETT. Because I'm good at prioritizing because I'm on top of my shit because I do all my homework in study hall and I do my extracurriculars in the mornings before school and so I just happen to have after-school free when you text –

JACK. So you're gonna be free to hang with me this summer?

EVERETT. Maybe I also have a secret girlfriend

JACK. Just bite my finger then we can hang

EVERETT. No

JACK. Because you don't want me to hang with Grace so you want to send me to piano camp even though I hate it

EVERETT. Because I don't want to bite off your fucking finger that's why

JACK. You want to punish me for having sex before you

EVERETT. If I wanted to have sex I would go have sex

JACK. Just like how if you wanted to watch porn you would watch porn but you don't?

EVERETT. Because it's bad for my understanding of women, I'm trying to be a feminist

JACK. Then bite my finger off if you love women so much

EVERETT. I love women. Like, all the time I love women

JACK. So you're not just trying to keep me away from my girlfriend?

EVERETT. I'm doing what any normal friend would do right now

JACK. Yeah but that's what I was trying to say
Like I know this is all new to you and shit but like
But sometimes I'm like
I can't tell if this is all a normal friendship desire that you have
Like if this is how it works for you
Or if like
I don't know bro
Or if like you might be a little bit like in –

EVERETT. Give me your finger.

> (**JACK** *extends his finger.* **EVERETT** *puts* **JACK**'s *finger in his mouth.*)

JACK. That's right just like a carrot

EVERETT. *(Mouth full.)* Yeah I fucking know I told you this

JACK. Come on do it

EVERETT. I'm gonna do it

JACK. Come on do it now

> (**EVERETT** *closes his mouth all the way over* **JACK**'s *finger. It's sort of tender for a moment.*)

Do you like my finger in your mouth

> (**EVERETT** *slowly shakes his head, unconvincing.*)

You do.

> (**EVERETT** *and* **JACK** *look into each other's eyes.*)

I don't think you're gonna bite my finger off.
Do you wanna know why?
Because I think you're in love –

> (**EVERETT** *bites* **JACK**'s *finger.*)

OW FUCK
OW FUCK LET GO

    (**EVERETT** *does not let go.*)

GOD FUCK LET FUCKING GO

    (**JACK** *tries to yank his finger out of* **EVERETT**'s *mouth.*)

STOP STOP I CHANGED MY MIND STOP

    (*A little blood drips out of* **EVERETT**'s *mouth.*)

YOU DON'T LOVE ME I WAS JUST BEING DUMB

    (**EVERETT** *releases* **JACK**'s *finger.*)

    (*They look at each other.*)

    (**JACK**'s *finger is bleeding, a lot.*)

    (*Beat.*)

EVERETT. You should go put some Neosporin on that.

JACK. Yeah. Okay.

    (**EVERETT** *resumes shooting hoops.*)

    (**JACK** *picks up his backpack to leave.*)

EVERETT. Have fun at piano camp.

JACK. Yeah. See ya.

    (**JACK** *leaves.*)

    (**EVERETT** *keeps shooting hoops.*)

    (*He keeps missing.*)

    (*He keeps missing.*)

    (*He keeps missing.*)

(Eventually, he gives up.)

(He sits down on the ground.)

(He puts his own finger in his mouth and closes his eyes.)

End of Play

2052

Gretchen Suárez-Peña

2052 was first produced by Theater Masters in New York City on April 26th, 2024. The performance was directed by victor cervantes jr. The cast was as follows:

ISOLDE ....Kelechi Nnamdi Udenkwo
TRICIA..Zuleyma Guevara
MAITE ....Shayvawn Webster

CHARACTERS

ISOLDE – male, American, late twenties. Searching. Paralysis of analysis. Maite's boyfriend. Tricia's co-worker and employee.

TRICIA – female, American, forties. Isolde's co-worker and boss. Holding down the fort. Always active.

MAITE – female, American, late twenties. A memory. Isolde's girlfriend. (Pronounced my-tay).

SETTING

A room with a desk in a modest home.
A dream or really a nightmare. An office.

TIME

2052

AUTHOR'S NOTES

Italics indicates a person speaks to themselves.

(**ISOLDE** *sits at a desk. The room is a mess – mostly clean unfolded laundry. He writes in a journal. We the audience are that journal. He speaks. Processes. Tries.)*

ISOLDE. Day 92.

Keep track.

I'm not sure if it's keeping me sane but numbers have always felt more grounding than emotions so…

We're down almost three billion.

The ash in the street is suffocating.

(Stops. Shakes head.)

Start over.

Recap.

The breadcrumbs will start to make sense.

It started with the solar flares.

Big ones that wrecked the grid. Two years ago.

It took like six months.

Six terrifying months, but we got back on track.

Technology fixed itself.

Things were going to be okay.

Better.

Then the cult started.

Cult?

Maite always called them a cult.

ISOLDE. *God, it hurts to write her name.*

They were a cult, she said.

A suicide cult.

TRICIA. *(Offstage.)* Isolde? You want coffee?

    *(**ISOLDE** thinks.)*

(Offstage.) Isolde?

ISOLDE. Yeah, sure!

TRICIA. *(Offstage.)* They had creamer at the bodega so…

ISOLDE. Okay!

    *(**ISOLDE** resumes.)*

Cult.

They said overpopulation was the biggest problem facing humanity.

No.

Climate change.

Maybe?

Kill yourself, they said.

So the world won't be overpopulated.

If you're wealthy and you've lived a good life.

Or, if your life sucked…

If you were old.

The more consumers die…the better.

Whatever it took.

They played on your guilt.

The solar flares were a sign, they said…

From God.

That humans needed to go.

Less carbon output…

The water would clean itself up.

Then came the opposition.

The Christians, the Buddhists, and other groups.

No, if you killed yourself, you'd go straight to hell.

Hell?

> *(Thinks.)*

This is hell.

The scientists said if too many people died then the decomposing bodies would emit more carbon.

What an argument to make.

Maite laughed.

> *(**TRICIA** enters with coffee.)*

TRICIA. Here you go.

ISOLDE. Thanks.

TRICIA. I'm gonna run the street sweeper today.

ISOLDE. You're damn good at keeping productive.

TRICIA. I can't be idle and I hate the ash. The wind has made everything from the crematorium come down Center Avenue. Have you seen the masks?

> *(**TRICIA** searches the room. Distracted with laundry, she starts to fold.)*

ISOLDE. I put them in the wash. They should be dry by now.

TRICIA. I'll be going by Silver Lake. You want me to stop by your place and get more of your stuff?

(**TRICIA** *tries to get* **ISOLDE** *to help with the laundry.* **ISOLDE** *ignores her gesture.*)

ISOLDE. No, I think I'm okay. Thanks again for letting me stay here.

TRICIA. As long as you need. It helps. To stay together. Have you called your dad?

ISOLDE. He called me, actually. My brother is coming in this week.

TRICIA. His wife?

ISOLDE. Yeah, her too, and the kids.

TRICIA. Good.

(*Considers him.*)

Javier wants to know if you want to join the neighborhood check-in brigade. It's just a once a week rotation. They need someone for Sunday nights.

ISOLDE. Talking to strangers? Really?

TRICIA. Even introverts need to do their part. It's helped keep losses at bay. People feel like they know their neighbors now. Like, they're less alone.

ISOLDE. I'll think about it.

TRICIA. You should do something.

ISOLDE. I'm not like you.

TRICIA. It's important to be part of the solution. I know they say you have to process things but sometimes you just have to keep moving.

(*Nods to the laundry.*)

Hands in motion. That's what keeps me going.

ISOLDE. My old therapist would say to be present. Mindful.

TRICIA. Yes, but present and doing. Living is active.

*(**ISOLDE** scoffs. **TRICIA** looks him over with maternal worry.)*

They want to open the office back up.

ISOLDE. They what? When?

TRICIA. Next month.

ISOLDE. Why? No one is hiring marketing companies.

TRICIA. The city just gave us a contract. An anti-death marketing campaign.

ISOLDE. Wow! Because that worked so well the last two years.

TRICIA. New tactics. Personal. Your designs will come in handy. You'll get paid.

ISOLDE. Humanity has succumbed to a death cult and capitalism prevails.

TRICIA. Some semblance of normalcy.

ISOLDE. Sure, boss. Whatever you say. It will be good for me, I guess. To keep busy.

TRICIA. I'll let them know then. I'll see you later.

*(**TRICIA** exits. A time shift.)*

*(**ISOLDE** resumes.)*

ISOLDE. Day 93

I've been thinking about Noah and the ark…

The cult always said that death would wash the earth clean.

Kill your family so they won't be alone without you.

It was real dark.

People justified the cause.

ISOLDE. Agreed.

Even if they weren't planning to join.

Let the crazies kill themselves.

More for the rest of us.

Maite said it was a passing trend.

Then it was kind of everywhere.

Graffiti.

Flyers at the grocery stores.

People wore emblems on their shirts.

January 1st, 2052.

That was the date.

They tried to stop it.

It would never happen, people said.

Then... Day 1.

(**MAITE** *enters. A memory.*)

MAITE. Isolde, they did it. Those people actually did it. They estimate 750,000 people died either by homicide or suicide.

ISOLDE. Day 2.

MAITE. Two million.

ISOLDE. Day 7.

MAITE. Twenty million.

ISOLDE. Day 14.

MAITE. One hundred million.

ISOLDE. Day 30.

MAITE. One billion.

ISOLDE. Every day.

   More and more people.

   Funeral homes couldn't keep up.

MAITE. We should eat.

ISOLDE. School was canceled.

   The economy halted.

MAITE. How'd you sleep last night?

ISOLDE. War stopped.

   Everything stopped.

MAITE. Today's numbers are in.

ISOLDE. Then Day 72 the numbers started tapering.

MAITE. Two billion, but this is the fourth straight day the new cases have dropped…ten percent they said.

ISOLDE. We kept track…

MAITE & ISOLDE. Together.

> *(**MAITE** disappears.)*

ISOLDE. That's all I can do now. Keep track.

> *(**ISOLDE** sits or lays down. Paralyzed. A time shift.)*

TRICIA. *(Offstage.)* Isolde? Isolde? You coming?

> *(**TRICIA** enters and sees him.)*

ISOLDE. I'm fine.

TRICIA. It's time for group.

ISOLDE. Nothing has changed since the last meeting.

TRICIA. It's good…

ISOLDE. To be around people. Yeah, I know. People just sit around and talk about the reasons why their family members ended their... They argue. Was it selfish or selfless? We're at early 2000s level population. They expect another billion will die in the next year based on trends.

TRICIA. I'm not so sure all this tracking is good for you. Please come.

ISOLDE. I'll go next week.

TRICIA. *(Relents. Redirects.)* I'm stopping by your place and getting you more stuff. I know you said you didn't need anything, but you've been wearing the same shirt all...

ISOLDE. I take showers.

TRICIA. Change your clothes, Isolde.

ISOLDE. Yeah, boss.

>   *(***TRICIA*** exits.* ***ISOLDE*** *goes back to his journal.)*

>   *(A time shift.)*

When Day 80 came, Maite was...

>   *(***MAITE*** *enters, a memory.)*

MAITE. Do you remember what sunshine looks like?

ISOLDE. Maite?

MAITE. It's so grey.

ISOLDE. The ash.

MAITE. I hate that smell.

ISOLDE. Me too. Are you okay?

MAITE. It's hard to laugh anymore. It was never a laughing matter, but we used to be happy...

ISOLDE. What can I do to make you smile?

MAITE. You don't have to do anything.

ISOLDE. Hey… I love you.

MAITE. I love you too.

ISOLDE. Then she was fine.

Back to normal.

I thought.

Then, day 85.

She was gone.

> (**MAITE** *disappears.*)

Most people left notes.

Had views you should worry about, but not Maite.

It's messing me up to not know why…

If I knew, then I could at least make sense of it.

Move forward.

I carried her to the crematorium.

There were forms to fill out.

Provide a reason for death.

But I have no clue.

Tricia manned the check-in process.

I hadn't seen her since before Christmas.

Tricia never took a break.

She offered me a place outside of my apartment.

Leaving your normal surroundings helped keep people alive.

ISOLDE. Grieve somewhere that didn't remind you of your loved ones.

I can understand the cultish, idealist, environmentalist, and depressed, but I can't understand Maite.

Everyone says that about their loved ones…

That they don't understand why they did it.

(Considers.)

Maite was always honest about how she felt.

She never hid…anything.

*(A time shift. A door opens offstage and jostles **ISOLDE**.)*

*(**TRICIA** enters with a box. She breaks the thoughts and brings us back to reality.)*

TRICIA. Hey, I brought some socks, shirts, pants. I figured you can go see your brother and dad tomorrow. My car has gas.

ISOLDE. Thanks. I should.

*(**TRICIA** stops. Considers. There is something really important in that box.)*

TRICIA. Isolde? I know Maite didn't leave a note, but… I found this…in the bathroom trash can.

*(**TRICIA** reveals a pregnancy test.)*

She was expecting.

ISOLDE. *(Loses it. Manic.)* No. No, that doesn't make any sense. She always wanted kids. Called them hope. Hope for the future. We needed hope now more than ever. She lost…hope. She didn't want to bring a child into this world. That has to be it. Damn cult. Damn solar flares. What am I supposed to do, Tricia? I know her reason, now. Right? She was pregnant. I don't know what to do with that information. I thought it would change... I could move forward if I knew but...

ISOLDE. (*Hysterics.*)   **TRICIA.**
Why are things like this?   Shhh. Shhhh. Shhh. It's okay. It's okay.

TRICIA. I want you to keep going. To live, but I can't choose that for you. I move. I help. I serve. That's what gives me purpose in all this... I want you to find that for yourself.

ISOLDE. (*Calms.*) You're right, boss. I know you're right.

    (*A moment. A hug. A consolation.*)

TRICIA. I'm gonna make some dinner. Okay?

    (**ISOLDE** *nods.*)

    (*A time shift.* **TRICIA** *hands* **ISOLDE** *the box. She exits.*)

ISOLDE. Day 99.

I don't look at the numbers anymore.

I emptied out the apartment.

I moved in with dad.

Tricia calls everyday.

I go back to work soon.

    (*A time shift.*)

Day 105

The sun came out through the grey this morning.

I smiled for the first time in months.

I went to work.

Tried to be present.

(A time shift.)

ISOLDE. Day 109

I've decided to be part of the solution – like Tricia said.

I'll never be as busy as her but…

I won't know how to move forward if I'm too scared to learn.

I've decided to move.

(A time shift.)

Day 120

I don't want to know the reasons of why there is death.

I don't want to know the numbers.

I joined the check-in brigade, and I ask people the reasons why they're still here.

The reasons to live.

The environment, they say.

To take care of their neighbors.

Take care of their dogs.

Take care of their parents or children.

Food.

Music.

To love again.

Somehow…learn to love again.

The Courtship Ritual of Sandhill Cranes

Emma Watkins

THE COURTSHIP RITUAL OF SANDHILL CRANES was first produced by Theater Masters in New York City on April 26th, 2024. The performance was directed by Julie Kramer. The cast was as follows:

VIVIAN .... Phyllis Yvonne Stickney
GEORGETTE .... Noa Graham

CHARACTERS

VIVIAN – Femme. A new docent at the "Heart of Texas" Natural History Museum.

GEORGETTE – Femme. An experienced docent at the "Heart of Texas" Natural History Museum.

AUTHOR'S NOTES

Vivian and Georgette can be played by femme actors of any age or race, provided that the actors are close in age.

(**VIVIAN** *walks onstage, her eyes closed, counting.*)

VIVIAN. 97. 98. 99. 100. Ready or not –

(She opens her eyes.)

(Blackout.)

(In darkness:)

VIVIAN & GEORGETTE. PREDATION IN THE DESERTS OF WEST TEXAS, A RED-TAILED HAWK DESCENDS UPON A JACKRABBIT.

(Lights up. A tableau.)

*(**VIVIAN** is crouched in the position of a small jackrabbit, looking innocently off into the distance.)*

*(Behind her, in the position of a diving hawk, is **GEORGETTE**.)*

(They are completely still as they speak this dialogue.)

GEORGETTE. The first thing the kids ask, when I'm taking them on a tour of the wildlife dioramas, is "Are those animals dead?"

VIVIAN. They're on their annual field trip to the "Heart of Texas" Museum of Natural History. And they've been patient through Rocks and Invertebrates and Weather Patterns. But I can tell which part they've been waiting for.

GEORGETTE. We make it to the diorama hall and they're – HEY. HEY. SLOW DOWN. DO NOT TOUCH THE GLASS.

VIVIAN. Come on everybody, gather in.

GEORGETTE. And then, the inevitable precocious little girl sticks up her hand: "Are those animals dead?"

VIVIAN. It's a great question, 'cause there is an obvious ethical dilemma here, with the taxidermy. 'Cause the animals *are* dead.

GEORGETTE. Of course, this question punctures the beauty of the dioramas, the spark of the almost-alive, the strange sensation of magically suspended time that the dioramas are working so hard to capture. It is a distracting question. So naturally, I deflect: "What we are looking at here is a red-tailed hawk, descending upon a jackrabbit."

VIVIAN. Because, right, what we're looking at here is two pelts, stretched over some wire and putty. It's the epitome of artificial. And actually, the reason there's glass between you and the taxidermy is that the whole thing has been treated with arsenic, to keep the bugs out. And you're right, the hawk isn't flying – it's suspended there, using fishing twine.

GEORGETTE. The problem is that no one believes in the magic of it anymore. I find it disheartening.

(Blackout.)

VIVIAN & GEORGETTE. THE COURTSHIP RITUAL OF SANDHILL CRANES

(Lights up. Tableau. We are in front of a new diorama.)

*(**VIVIAN** and **GEORGETTE** are sandhill cranes, engaged in an elaborate, entirely still, mating ritual.)*

GEORGETTE. Whenever I am leading a particularly deadbeat tour, I comfort myself by remembering that the museum's Holiday Sleepover Party is just a few days away. The Holiday Sleepover Party is the best part about being a docent.

VIVIAN. To be clear, they've put up a flyer asking for two volunteers to chaperone the Holiday Sleepover Party, which is intended for local middle-schoolers.

GEORGETTE. It is the most wonderful time of the year.

VIVIAN. It says volunteers will lead a variety of educational games –

GEORGETTE. And then a museum-wide game of hide-and-go-seek!

The best hiding place in the museum is a well-kept secret. It's the American Bison diorama. People don't know this, but the lock on the door to the bison diorama is broken, so it doesn't lock, don't tell anyone this, but the lock on the door is broken so you can go inside the diorama. And stand behind the bison. And be very very very still. It's the best hiding spot.

VIVIAN. Word on the street is that there's one docent, one maybe rather odd docent, who takes the hide-and-go-seek more seriously than everyone else.

GEORGETTE. I have never been found.

> *(Blackout.)*

VIVIAN & GEORGETTE. SPARRING BETWEEN PRONGHORNS IN THE HIGH PLAINS OF THE TEXAS PANHANDLE

> *(Lights up. Tableau:* **GEORGETTE** *and* **VIVIAN** *are pronghorns, about to collide with one another. They are completely still.)*

VIVIAN. Have you noticed that wildlife dioramas always capture the moment Right Before something happens? Something extraordinary? Right Before the pronghorns crash their antlers together. Right Before the sandhill cranes finish their elaborate courtship ritual. I've noticed that a disproportionate number of dioramas capture the moment Right Before killing or sex. Sorry, I mean, copulation. I mean, courtship.

GEORGETTE. I feel like I spend most of my time in the moment Right Before.

VIVIAN. But I guess it speaks to our fascination, right, our visceral fascination, with the moment Right Before. When it's all anticipation, but no substance, not yet.

GEORGETTE. I suspect it's because when I'm flirting, I get very excited, and then I get very anxious.

VIVIAN. That's why I became a docent at the natural history museum. I love dioramas. Because in that perfect, arsenic stillness, you can study the moment Right Before, in a way that you never get to, not in real life. You can look at it, carefully – try to see what you missed the first time around.

(Blackout.)

VIVIAN & GEORGETTE. TWO VOLUNTEER DOCENTS IN THE STAFF ROOM OF THE "HEART OF TEXAS" MUSEUM OF NATURAL HISTORY ON THE DAY OF THE HOLIDAY SLEEPOVER PARTY.

(Lights up. Tableau: **VIVIAN** *and* **GEORGETTE** *are in the fluorescent-lit staff room.* **VIVIAN** *sits at the table.* **GEORGETTE** *leans authoritatively against the counter, holding coffee. They are completely still.)*

GEORGETTE. The kids won't want to be "It." We always give them the option, but they prefer to hide.

VIVIAN. Right.

GEORGETTE. But of course, someone has to be "It." Usually one of the chaperones.

VIVIAN. I don't mind being "It."

GEORGETTE. That's amazing, thank you, so you can be "It." Your name is Vivian, right?

VIVIAN. Yeah.

GEORGETTE. That's great, thank you Vivian. I'm Georgette. Thank you for volunteering. Thank you for being here. Sincerely.

VIVIAN. Of course.

GEORGETTE. Oftentimes, the other docents, they don't sign up to chaperone the Holiday Sleepover Party. Oftentimes, it's just me. So it's nice, it's really nice, to have someone volunteer.

VIVIAN. Yeah. Happy to.

GEORGETTE. Oftentimes, people don't have your attitude. It's great, to have an attitude like yours. Are you enjoying it here so far?

VIVIAN. Oh yeah, I think it's great.

GEORGETTE. It's great, isn't it? I love it here. Has Charlotte given you the behind-the-scenes tour? Charlotte's the Museum Director. You've met Charlotte, right?

VIVIAN. Yeah, she was at orientation.

GEORGETTE. You should ask her, Charlotte gives a great behind-the-scenes tour, she's got lots of fun facts, and they're great, 'cause then you can put the best fun facts into your tour. Like little Easter Eggs. It's great, 'cause that way you can reward the people who are really paying attention. Like you. I can tell you're the kind of person who really pays attention.

VIVIAN. I like to think so.

GEORGETTE. So do you want to know my best fun fact? It's a secret.

VIVIAN. Oh. Yeah! Sure, I guess.

GEORGETTE. OK, follow me.

VIVIAN. Oh.

GEORGETTE. It's a site-specific secret.

(Blackout.)

VIVIAN & GEORGETTE. TWO VOLUNTEER DOCENTS STAND IN FRONT OF A DIORAMA CALLED "THE COURTSHIP RITUAL OF SANDHILL CRANES"

(Lights up. Tableau: **VIVIAN** *and* **GEORGETTE** *are standing in front of the sandhill crane diorama.* **GEORGETTE** *is pointing. They are completely still.)*

GEORGETTE. Can you tell which one is which?

VIVIAN. How do you mean?

GEORGETTE. Which bird's the guy, which one's the girl?

VIVIAN. Well. That one's a little bit bigger.

GEORGETTE. Yep, mhm.

VIVIAN. So maybe that one's the male?

GEORGETTE. You'd think so.

VIVIAN. So it's the other one?

GEORGETTE. Nope.

VIVIAN. What do you mean?

GEORGETTE. So, when the museum ordered the cranes, from a hunter out in Abilene, this is in 1915, but the hunter screwed up, and sent the museum two *female* cranes, instead of one male, one female, like they'd asked for. But it was too late, it was too close to the museum's grand opening, so the museum director just stuck both of the lady cranes inside the diorama, and just hoped no one would notice. For the most part, people don't notice.

VIVIAN. Wow.

GEORGETTE. That's my best fun fact. Here, in the "Heart of Texas" Museum of Natural History, we've got two gay cranes. I mean, lesbian cranes. I mean, queer.

VIVIAN. Wow.

GEORGETTE. But don't include that fun fact on your tour.

VIVIAN. Oh. Of course.

GEORGETTE. 'Cause once, I included it on the tour, and a dad got mad and took his kids away from the tour. So I save it. It's a fun fact I save for myself. And for people who I can tell will get it, get the museum, who I think will really appreciate it.

(Beat.)

So, um. There ya go.

VIVIAN. Thank you for telling me.

GEORGETTE. I just think they're pretty neat.

VIVIAN. Super cool. Thank you.

GEORGETTE. Have you seen sandhill cranes do their courtship ritual?

VIVIAN. You mean in real life? No. I haven't.

GEORGETTE. It's great. They're so awkward. They kind of – throw themselves into the air and make a bububadabada sound. It's not flying. More like hopping. They just look surprised. And then happy. To see each other.

(Beat.)

(A sound in the distance – a humming, growing louder.)

VIVIAN. What's that?

GEORGETTE. The school busses must be here.

VIVIAN. Wow, it's quite loud.

GEORGETTE. The children get very excited.

VIVIAN. Should we go throw a holiday party then?

GEORGETTE. Oh, I think we should.

(Blackout.)

(The sound of the museum whirring back to life: children running, being told to stop running, chaos, echoes, laughing.)

*(Lights slowly come up on **VIVIAN** as she's counting.)*

VIVIAN. 1, 2. 3.

It's weird, being in the museum, after hours. After the sun has gone down. Weird being in this cavernous old space. Eyes closed. I hear the kids, hiding. Little feet, lots of little feet, running away from me. They're whispering. They're negotiating. They're choosing hiding places. Squeezing into their hiding spaces. Holding still.

17. 18.

The museum gets quieter. And quieter. Until you could hear a pin drop.

34, 35, 36.

So upon closer study. Of the moment Right Before this moment. Because…was she maybe flirting with me?

That thing about gay sandhill cranes? I mean lesbian. I mean queer.

That's what flirting looks like. Right?

Or that's what flirting looks like if you're a volunteer docent at the "Heart of Texas" Museum of Natural History. God she's such a dork. She's such a cute dork.

Only one way to find out. Uck. Terrifying.

72 73 74 75 76

'Cause I could, I could spend the whole rest of my whole life looking through a nice piece of glass, protecting myself from whatever's on the other side, 'cause there could be something on the other side, something arsenic – but am I really gonna spend the rest of my life like that? Commenting on the artifice. Looking in.

And she seems actually…kind of sweet.

99.

Oh god.

READY OR NOT –

(Blackout.)

VIVIAN & GEORGETTE. THE AMERICAN BISON

(Lights up.)

*(On the other side of the stage, **GEORGETTE** has appeared. She is hiding behind the bison, standing very very very still. **VIVIAN** walks towards her.)*

VIVIAN. Because life isn't, it can't be, holding still, petrified, forever, take a risk, MOVE, damn it, stop analyzing. Just do the thing, just do the thing, Vivian, you should do it, you should say it, say it, say, say, say –

I found you.

*(**GEORGETTE** turns around, looks at her.)*

(They walk toward each other.)

*(**VIVIAN** and **GEORGETTE** perform the mating ritual of the sandhill cranes: flapping, hopping, legs at weird angles.)*

(Bububadabada.)

(It's awkward and beautiful and strange.)

(They get closer and closer, until they are about to kiss.)

(Blackout.)

The End

www.ingramcontent.com/pod-product-compliance
Lightning Source LLC
Chambersburg PA
CBHW051455290426
44109CB00016B/1761